PACK THE HOUSE !

The Ultimate, Ever-Growing Guide to Increasing Attendance at YOUR On-Campus Events

By C.J. Johnson
and Brian Brushwood

Cover photo by Scott Hylton

Printed in the United States of America

ISBN 0-9713646-1-3

First Printing, 2000

Introduction

Welcome to our book! We hope you not only enjoy it, but put the ideas to use in promoting your on-campus events. Most of the examples in this book came from things that we've seen used successfully on college campuses during the past few years. These ideas are not "pipe dreams" but practical, inexpensive, and often times FREE ways to promote your events. Remember that both the performer and the activities committee benefits from a good crowd. Selecting the best entertainment in the college market is useless unless students know the act will be there. This book will help you let them know in original, creative, and outrageous ways.

Since not all schools are the same, some of the ideas won't be useful to you directly (but many more will). Our hope is that these examples will get your creative juices flowing and will help you "Pack the House" at all of your special events.

We do not consider this book to be complete by any means, and if you have any great ideas we'd love to include them in the next edition. You can E-mail them to us through our web site www.WeLoveNACA.com and we'll give your school credit for the creativity.

Brian Brushwood
and
C.J. Johnson

1.

MAKE IT

Real

The more clearly your students can visualize your event, the more likely they'll be to come. Whenever possible, take objects, ideas, and visuals from the upcoming event and do everything in your power to implant them in your crowd's mind.

EXAMPLES:

✔　　The University of St. Thomas was promoting an act that had a fire eater, so they gave away atomic fireballs with the message attached: "Think these are hot? Try eating FIRE!" Later, the fire eater used the same gimmick to get on "The Roseanne Show," and later "Talk Soup."

✔　　For a juggler, assemble a collection of the types of objects he will be juggling, such as a bowling ball, knives, pins, fruit, etc. Make sure to attach a message saying what he'll do with them.

✔　　Again, when promoting their bizarre magician, the University of St. Thomas placed 30-pound concrete bricks around campus with the message attached: "Watch a bizarre magician break these over his head!"

2. MAKE IT

Ever-Present

There is a popular maxim in advertising that people will view an ad **six times** before they pay any attention to it. If you've put up one or two posters in the commons and think you're done, *you're in trouble*! Your advertising needs to be so ever-present, you can't stand <u>anywhere</u> on campus and *not* see at least one ad.

If you're unhappy with attendance at your events, you can often double attendance simply by doubling the number of advertisements you make!

EXAMPLES:

✔   Fliers. They're cheap, plentiful, easy, and hands down your best tool for representing your event. Place them **everywhere**. In bathroom stalls, on kiosks, on doorways, hallways, walkways, ceilings, floors, and anywhere else you can reach. These are the quickest way to make multiple impressions. Remember that students judge how big an event is **directly** upon the number of advertisements they **see**.

✔   Chalk stencils. Make a series of arrows all over campus that lead to your event. Remember that ever-present means just that: even the floors are potential advertising space. It's different, and will go a long way to making an impression on your students

✔   Banners. Size matters! Grab some butcher paper and paint, and go to town. Banners are cheap, easy, and do the job of a billboard.

✔   Table Tents. Just like restaurants, you have a captive audience during mealtimes. Set up tri-fold or bi-fold table tents with plenty of copy (that's advertising talk for "words") selling the event. If someone's eating alone, they often have nothing else to do. That person may read your entire sales pitch and decide right there that they will attend!

Making table tents is a snap! Here are two templates for tri-fold and bi-fold table tents:

Tri-Fold table tent example:

Bi-Fold table tent example:

Tri-Fold table tent template:

Bi-Fold table tent template:

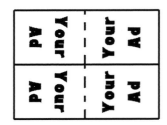

3. MAKE IT EASY

Not everything you do has to be built from scratch. Save yourself valuable brain power and time by asking your act for promotional materials. They've been doing this a long time, and probably have a pretty good idea about what works. They can provide you with:

EXAMPLES:

✔ **Pictures** - such as 8x10 glossies suitable for reproduction.

✔ **"FAQ" sheet** - This list of "Frequently Asked Questions" will help you address many of your act's most common concerns. The better you know your act, the better you can promote it.

✔ **Letters of Recommendation** - by reading what others have said about the show, you give yourself a powerful arsenal of testimonial quotes. Let these quotes show up in your advertising.

✔ **Fliers** - make sure that you get posters and fliers from the act you are working with, and be sure to keep one original around just in case you need to make reprints.

✔ **Video footage** - you can run these on monitors in high

traffic areas, and at meals. Attach to the monitors a message detailing the act and the event.

✔ **Clip art and action shots** - Use the Internet to gather clip art and photos for your own designs. In today's market many, if not most, acts have web sites. You can use these to grab pictures, graphics and biographical information to create your own fliers and posters.

✔ **Press releases** - these are filled with promotional texts that can save you hours of tough thinking (ouch). Take advantage of their efforts and spend yours on implementation.

. . . Strangely enough, most press releases end up printed in newspapers exactly as they are given, or with only minor changes. The key point to getting your press release printed is to make it a **news** item. Find an angle that makes it news, not just a way to promote your event.

✔ Most acts will be thrilled to give you any promotional materials they have. Remember that having a good crowd is just as important to **them** as it is for **you**. After all, a bigger crowd equals a better show.

4. MAKE IT MYSTERIOUS

This one's pretty universal. You've probably seen it used for movies, new product releases, new advertising campaigns--anything that can be "unveiled."

The idea is simple: create interest by refusing to give out details. Ten years ago, computer chip maker Intel heralded the release of their new 386 chipset by simply putting up billboards with the numbers "286" with a big "X" through them. The Batman movie relied on mysterious billboards featuring the bat-logo.

In 1985, many college campuses found chalk graffiti stenciled everywhere. Each stencil read the same: "Turk 182." Confusion on campus grew until billboard advertisements revealed the upcoming release of "Turk 182," a movie *about* graffiti.

Recently Service Lane (a company that specializes in service professionals) ran a series of billboards for fake moving and cleaning services like "D. Crepit movers" and "Misty Meanor Maids." After confusion built up, they unveiled new boards with the slogan "if all service ads were this clear, you wouldn't need us!"

Here's your general rule of thumb: if it makes someone stop and say "what's that all about?" Then it probably is doing it's job. Folks will check in on it later, and eventually **notice** what it's all about!

EXAMPLES:

✔   Several years ago at Texas A&M university, one candidate for student elections violated university policy by hanging up large banner posters before the official campaign start date. Although many students wanted the banners taken down, this student argued that he would be relinquishing valuable advertising real estate, as he had placed his ads in several prime locations. Therefore, the faculty agreed that rather than take down his banners, he was to cover them up until the official start date.

Our hero did as he was told, covering up each large poster so they could not be read. However, in a stroke of genius, he stenciled the simple words "coming soon" on each covering. One week later **all of campus** was wondering what could possibly be under the "coming soon" covers!

✔   You can use a derivative of the "coming soon" idea by revealing a poster a little bit at a time. Make sure that the answer to "what's this all about" is revealed last.

✔   In high-traffic areas where people have extra time to kill (such as the cafeteria), you can actually make your advertisement into a puzzle. Print a large "encoded" message, along with a "key," or perhaps do a word jumble. Making your ad a fun challenge to understand can vastly increase the amount of time your students spend thinking about it.

5. MAKE IT

Controversial

Wherever there's conflict, there's crowds. In the 1950's, one hypnotist would actually hire protesters to stir up a fuss the week before his show, claiming hypnosis was immoral. They would get tons of media coverage, and then the hypnotist would show up and say "I don't know what all this fuss is about. Why don't you come, see the show, and judge for yourself!"

He always played to packed houses.

You, too can do this same thing, either as a serious hoax, or as an obvious parody. It's up to you how far you take it. Remember that the controversy doesn't have to be biting, and that at it's best it will be ludicrous. Having a ridiculous figurehead helps with this a lot!

To some extent, this is exactly what magicians Penn and Teller did to increase their notoriety. They invented stories that magicians hated them wanted them shut down. It made great patter for the show, but to their surprise, such magicians really began to show up! Protests were made, petitions were signed, and Penn and Teller quickly rose to stardom.

Here's a more subtle approach: One hypnotist paid a man to spread conflicting rumors about hypnosis, just to generate conversation. He'd tell one person, "I hear there's this great hypnotist coming in to town," and to the next he'd say "I hear hypnosis is really of the devil!"

Try forming your own fake protest group, and:

EXAMPLES:

✔   Demand the banning of hypnosis because it's "immoral mind control."

✔   Claim a magician is in league with the forces of darkness.

✔   Claim a comedian violates the rights of the ugly people.

✔   Residents of Kansas have a rare opportunity to stir up REAL controversy: since 1969, Kansas has kept hypnosis shows illegal! Under Article 40, section 21-4007, "Hypnotic Exhibition" (basically defined as participating in a hypnosis show) is a misdemeanor punishable by a fine not to exceed (get ready) . . . $50.

Many entertainers circumvent this law by performing "hypno-mentalism" shows instead of "hypnosis" shows, but YOU can use this law to mount a campaign about ANY performer, claiming he or she causes a "hypnotic" effect on you!

6. MAKE IT

Public

Free publicity is **pure gold** to event promoters. You can tap into your own share of this lode by doing anything that gets news media attention. Create photo opportunities for your school newspaper (or the local town newspaper, for that matter) to capture and use. Stage a "welcome party" for your performer. All you need is a bunch of excited programming council members and a big sign welcoming your act, and your set. The event may not seem like much to you, but it creates a visual moment that all forms of news media can latch on to. It's a mental and physical picture they can print!

You don't need to stop there, though. Create a parade or circus atmosphere as you hand out information about the show. Not only is this perfect to grab the attention of the media, but it allows you to make a much greater impression on everyone you tell the event to. In fact, when the Bindlestiff Family Cirkus hands out fliers on campuses advertising their shows, they make sure each one is lit **on fire!** Not only was this a great photo opportunity, but the students **definitely** took notice.

EXAMPLES:

✔   Parade around in advertising sandwich boards handing out information about the show. Media will cover this the way they cover politicians campaigning (and for good reason--you're both doing the same job!).

✔   Have a student perform some wacky feat (unicycling, juggling, pogo sticking... anything that makes a good photo) and hand out information.

✔   Try a marching or strolling jazz or mariachi band. Hand out fliers as you parade around.

✔   Make sure you have a media representative present at every teaser you do! There's no reason they shouldn't take advantage of the free story, or that you shouldn't take advantage of the free publicity.

✔   If you're having trouble getting an article written about your event, remember that there's a close relationship between advertisers and articles. It just so happens that most acts who get "fluff" pieces written about them ALSO advertise with the paper.

✔   The general rule is this: create an angle of public interest (not just an advertisement), then stage an event that makes the perfect picture.

7.

MAKE IT

Regular

Remember: You're in marketing.

For years EVERYONE knew what was on NBC at 8:00 Thursday nights. Seinfeld became a permanent, regular fixture in the minds of the TV viewing public, thanks largely to NBC's "Must See TV Thursday" campaigns. You can make the same idea work for you.

You can generate much better crowds if everyone on campus knows that every single Tuesday, there's a great act coming to campus at your auditorium. Give it a name. Make it regular. Make sure it's solid as a rock, so people can depend on seeing a great, free show every week, month, semester or year.

In other words, instead of "Harry Hypnotist will be here Nov. 8th!" (a one time event), everyone could know that "next weeks 'wig-out Wednesday' will feature harry hypnotist!" See the difference? One is an isolated event whose success will be entirely dependant on the draw of

Harry Hypnotist, while the other, is a description of this weeks special feature--part of a regular campaign!

One great example of this tactic is Southwest Texas University's "CricketFest." Every year, San Marcos, TX. is blighted by millions of crickets. By theming an event around this phenomenon, SWT has guaranteed that every time a student sees hundreds of crickets, they know that CricketFest is near!

EXAMPLES:

✔   Own a certain date or weekday in the public's mind. keep it simple, but direct. Make sure the necessary information is built into the event's title.

✔   Each event can be so much more than the act itself. You can ADD VALUE by offering regular features like giveaways, contests, games and more.

✔   This kind of adding value also allows you to stretch a comedian's 40 minute presentation into a 90 minute show! PLUS, extras before the show will build anticipation for the main event, helping to ensure the performance's success!

8. MAKE IT
Current

By referencing current pop culture, you're able to take a thought already on someone's mind, and use it as a "peg" to hang your advertisement on. This is most effective as a way to GET NOTICED.

EXAMPLES:

✔   In your advertising, spoof current popular ads (the taco bell Chihuahua, Jack, the mountain dew guys, etc.).

✔   In your events, add an extra segment that allows students to play spoofs of popular game shows. Northwestern State university in Natchitoches, Louisiana made a spoof game show called "who wants to win $100.00?"

✔   In your advertising, reference issues that are relevant and up to date. These can be major news items that JUST came out, or campus issues that are on everyone's minds.

9. MAKE IT FUNNY

When people hear a great joke, they share it with everyone they can. The joke spreads, almost like an infection. Imagine what could happen if you used the same phenomenon to spread the word about your event? Do your best to make sure your advertising is clever, witty, or outrageous. The funnier the better!

How many times have you described an advertisement to your friends that you found particularly cute or funny? Each time you do this, you're providing an additional (and better) advertisement for the product. The amazing part is that these thousands and thousands of extra hidden ads are FREE!

Remember: your goal is to be so funny that everyone who sees it will want to tell their friends about it.

10.

MAKE IT

Specific

Instead of trying to explain whole acts, shows, concerts, or themes on a single poster, try extrapolating a single event from the show, and advertise as though that alone were the only reason to go see it. This works best if you have a series of posters, each one in the same style, touting different individual aspects of the show. This will help feed the word of mouth advertising by causing people to mention things like "did you hear about the act tonight? I hear he's going to juggle live hamsters!"

You can make these statements simple or complex, positive or negative, mysterious or up front. The purpose is merely to get folks thinking.

EXAMPLES:

✔   For a Hypnotist: "What happens when a man loses everything he owns?" "See Michael Jackson, Madonna, and Elvis LIVE ON OUR STAGE!" "See someone forget their own name." "If nobody remembers the number 7, does it exist?" "Hear a special Lecture from Steve Irwin, the Crocodile Hunter."

✔   For a bizarre magician: "Watch a grown man stick a nail in his eye." "What this guy break a 30 lb. brick over his head." "See your roommate have her mind read." "Learn some bets you can't lose." "You might be the one to strap this guy into a straitjacket."

✔   For jugglers: "Is it even possible to juggle five balls at once?" "How much weight can you balance on YOUR chin?" "Come see the tallest unicycle ever ridden on campus."

✔   For comedians: "Find out why dysfunctional families are funny." "Straight from 'The Late Show' to our auditorium" Make sure to tailor your ads to each comedian's presentation and credentials.

11. MAKE IT

COUNTER-INTUITIVE

"Reverse Ads" take advantage of people's inherent desire to not do what they're told. For obvious reasons, they work exceptionally well with college students. In Austin, Texas, one particularly successful billboard featured the following message in black stencil on a plain white background: "DO NOT LISTEN TO 107.1 KGSR." Every person driving by the billboard immediately tuned in to find out what all the fuss is about. Most stayed when they realized it was a pretty great station.

Remember: you want students to question your statements. The more broad and certain it is, the more likely they will be to question it and show up.

EXAMPLES:

✔ "Hypnosis does not exist."

✔ "Billy Comedian is not funny"

✔ "Sticking a nail in your eye is no big deal"

✔ "This famous band does not rock"

12. MAKE IT Ever-Changing

How many times have you walked into a friend's apartment an immediately noticed that the furniture has been rearranged? Or that he just put up a new poster? Or that he cut his hair? Or is wearing a new shirt?

The human eye is exceptionally good at noticing differences (though we may sometimes miss our loved one's makeovers). You can use this fact to make your posters and advertisements more noticeable. Create an advertising campaign based on your ads changing every single day. People will notice. People will talk. This is exactly what you want.

EXAMPLES:

✔   Posters that read "X more days until Johnny Comic comes to campus."

✔   Imagine a mannequin holding a poster advertising your event. Now imagine the interest when every single day, one more piece of clothing seems to disappear from it. THAT should catch some interest.

✔   A particularly noticeable poster moves to a different location in the cafeteria every single day. Sometimes it's on the wall, the floor, a table, the ceiling, upside down, or hanging from the flagpole.

✔   Posters that slowly become defaced with drawn-on glasses, goatees, etc. This could lead to a news story about your defaced posters... and to free publicity for your event.

13. MAKE IT Irresistible

Here is the simplest way to guarantee capacity crowds for every event you have for the rest of your tenure: present your case for attendance as expertly as any high-priced defense lawyer would present his. In other words, treat your students as a jury, who must be absolutely convinced that your event will be so great that they would be a **complete fool** to miss out on it.

EXAMPLES:

✔   Use "apples to oranges" comparisons to explain the tremendous value available to students. For instance: "Why go to a comedy club and pay 15 dollars PLUS overpriced food to see Johnny Comic when you can see him and enjoy pizza here absolutely free!"

✔   Use the same reasons that convinced you to hire your act to sell it your students. "Hypnosis Harry won 'campus entertainer of the year' 6 YEARS RUNNING! Find out why on Thursday night!"

✔   Statistics: "Over 30,000 students went to see The Amazing Mysterio last year. Find out WHY!"

✔   Elvis Presley had an album that proclaimed "100 Million Elvis fans can't be wrong!" It's flawed logic, but it sold records.

14. MAKE IT "HOLLYWOOD"

How you depict your act directly determines how your act is perceived on campus both before and after the show.

Therefore, you have a vested interest in making everything about your act seem like the world's greatest celebrity. If your students believe they are lucky to even have the chance to see such a star, they will make a much greater effort to turn out for the event. Even better is the fact that once they're there, they'll be more respectful, more attentive, and have a much better time.

It doesn't matter if your act has celebrity status or not. If you don't tell your students how lucky they are to have them, they won't know!

EXAMPLES:

✔   Quote accolades for your act on every bit of promotional material. These can be awards they've won, attendance statistics, quotes from media sources, and more. Again, the odds are good that your act has already provided you with these.

✔   Never underestimate the power of "as seen on..." After all, if they've appeared on national television, they have to be famous, right?

✔   You can help build the perception of an act's celebrity by creating a media event surrounding the act's arrival. A television, radio, or newspaper spot showing fans awaiting the act's arrival can't help but build anticipation.

15.

This is the flipside of number 14.

In addition to convincing your students that your act is a celebrity, do everything you can to make your act *feel* like a celebrity.

Every professional entertainer always does the best he can at every show. But just how good his best can be is directly affected by negative factors like fatigue, frustration, hunger, time issues, venue issues, a botched practice, last minute changes, jet lag, sound and lighting issues, and his overall sense of being appreciated. Put simply: if you act notices that you've gone the extra mile to make him feel appreciated, then he will go the extra mile to make sure yours is the very best show he can do.

If you having trouble believing this, consider the two following scenarios:

EXAMPLES:

✔   In scenario #1, The Amazing Mysterio arrives on campus to find 8 programming council members waiting at the theatre, all dressed in matching university T-shirts. They offer to help him load in, they make sure the tech crew is present and ready for a sound and light rehearsal. Mysterio is treated to a welcome basket of drinks and snacks, and is presented with a special gift of a university mug and T-shirt.

✔   In scenario #2, Mysterio shows up on campus and has to ask students where the programming council office is, since he was given no specific venue. When he finds them, everyone in the PC acts as though where to have the show just occurred to them. Mysterio is then squeezed into the cafeteria, where he spends 30 minutes rearranging tables to create a makeshift stage. Once Mysterio begins his show, the two or three PC members stick around for 10 or 15 minutes, then disappear, never to be seen again.

In which of these scenarios will Mysterio be at peak performance?

Remember, how well the show goes is just as much up to your preparation as your act's execution.

16. MAKE IT

Valued

Remember: something free has no value. It's important that you create the illusion of scarcity and value for your event.

EXAMPLES:

✔ Require reservations and tickets for the event (even though it's free). By having reservation and ticket booths around campus, you take the student's decision to attend the event and "crystallize" it by requiring he sign up and get a ticket to attend. This also will give you an accurate measure in advance of how well the event will do.

✔ Although you're not charging money, make sure to collect demographic information to better help you know your audience. This will allow you to custom-tailor future promotions.

17. MAKE IT

Personal

Remember: your job is not to say why **you** chose this act. Your job is to tell them why **they** should come to it. Make statements that will speak to your students concerns.

EXAMPLES:

✔   "It's a Cheap Date."

✔   "'The Simpsons' is a rerun this week!"

✔   "The internet will still be there when you get home."

✔   "Ditch your roommate for an evening!"

✔   "Skip the ramen noodles, get some free pizza!"

18. MAKE IT V.I.P.

If you have regular programming council events, there's value in making your "regulars" feel appreciated. For one, it will keep them being a "regular."

Take a hint from car rental agencies, airlines, and sandwich shops. Establish some form of "rewards" program to keep people coming. Try giving your students a reason besides the act to come.

EXAMPLES:

✔ Establish a V.I.P. section in your auditorium, reserved for those with a sufficient number of "punches" in their campus activity card.

✔ Offer a special prize for anyone attending "all 8 events" this year.

✔ Pass around a signup sheet for a free drink and slice of pizza at next week's event (only collectible if they attend).

✔ Offer your V.I.P. section to the best-represented dorm or the dorm with the best promotion.

✔   In Raleigh, North Carolina, Cort Furniture sponsors a special V.I.P. section at all arena football games. The section is offered as a special prize to the lucky individuals who win a random drawing. In the V.I.P. section, winners are treated to snacks, drinks, and (of course) big, plush easy chairs provided by Cort furniture!

19.

Wearable

Concert T-shirts aren't just fashionable ways to prove you saw "so-and-so" live, they're walking billboards! Make clothing or accessories to advertise your event. There are ways to do this that will fit virtually any budget, including:

EXAMPLES:

✔   Special event-specific T-shirts that the Programming Council or general student body wear that advertise upcoming events. At each event, you can give away a few T-shirts that advertise your next event.

✔   Make a set of 10 T-shirts that simply say "Big Event

Tonight: Ask Me for Details." Have your team wear them the day of each of your events.

✔   Make buttons. Custom button-making machines are less than $40, and the cost-per-button is under $.25! You can even have random giveaways on campus that are only available to someone wearing a promotional button!

✔   You can even make iron-on transfers for T-shirts using your own computer. These shirts can be as cheap as $3 each!

20. MAKE IT Impossible

The creation of an 'impossibility' or visually interesting phenomenon will get people talking. Tying in an endorsement channels that conversation to your benefit.

A few years ago I attended a magic convention at a 25-story tall hotel. From the inner courtyard, everyone could see all the way up to the top of the building. A fast-growing topic of conversation was what appeared to be magic wand "floating" ten stories up, in the middle of the hotel. It turns out that a magician had tied two strands of invisible thread to two cleverly hidden places and created the illusion.

Your advertisement can be a topic of conversation, if you place it in an impossible location.

EXAMPLES:

✔   Place a banner advertisement on the 25-foot ceiling of your cafeteria. Odds are good no one's seen that before.

✔   Create a visual oddity, like the floating wand. Maybe a floating mannequin? Or a glowing sign?

✔   Go wild! Think up some modern art projects to which you can attach your information. Different is good.

21. MAKE IT CROSS-PROMOTIONAL

Use the strength of corporate America to bolster your attendance. The idea of cross-promotion is simple: you scratch my back; I'll scratch yours. Simply by partnering with a local business, you can trade endorsements for foods, goods, and promotions.

Remember, too, that your cross-promotions don't have to be with outside businesses. You can cross promote with the cafeteria, the lecture series, even particular classes!

EXAMPLES:

If you were to partner with your local pizza shop, you could:

✔ In exchange for publicity, have them send out fliers for your events with each pizza delivered on campus. Also have them place your ads in their shop windows.

✔ Schedule giveaways of pizza coupons at your event in exchange for mutual advertising.

✔ Offer discounts at the pizza shop for anyone with a ticket stub from last week's event. Or better yet. . .

✔ Offer discounts for anyone with a ticket for **next** week's event. This way, your tickets (although free) have inherent value beyond the show.

If you cross promote on campus:

✔ Tie-in your event with the lunch menu. It doesn't matter if the tie-in makes sense, as long as people notice it.

✔ Hand out pamphlets for the University Health Center, and in exchange, have them put up your posters.

✔ Offer free drinks at your event to anyone bringing in an overdue library book to your event, and in exchange have the library hand out your flier with each book checked out.

✔   Place door hangers on each door at the dorm. This works especially well if you include a coupon for one of your corporate partners.

✔   Don't forget to extend offers and invitations to the Greeks!

22. MAKE IT "Right There"

This sounds obvious, but for some reason, nobody takes advantage of it: Every single act, regardless of it's nature can do some kind of teaser. Yet you'd be amazed how few people take advantage of this.

Teasers can pull in students who had no idea the event was coming up, or better yet, those who had previously decided not to go to the event. Teasers give students a real taste of the act right there in front of them. In my experience, a single teaser can bring 20 to 40 people to the show that night.

Don't think your act is right for teasers? Think again. Anyone can do a teaser even if it's just one of these:

EXAMPLES:

✔   Hold an autograph signing

✔   Hold a Question and Answer forum

✔   Personally introduce your act and have him walk around the cafeteria shaking hands (the way politicians do).

✔   If you book an on-campus act (like the university juggling club) to open for "the big show," (say, a hypnotist) your teaser can be the on-campus act! This allows you to visually grab everyone's attention, and then say "think these guys are good? They're just the opening act for Mr. Bigshot Hypnotist!"

23. MAKE IT
"a promotions machine"

The best way to keep attendance up is to create a "promotions machine" that works, and then keep doing it. In other words, rather than try to think up new advertising campaigns for each act, find a single set of "general tactics," and adapt them to each show.

Here's a short list of "must-dos" to keep your promotion

machine working:

EXAMPLES:

✔   Start and maintain an E-mail list. Simply pass around a clipboard at each event and collect the email of everyone present. Now, before each event, you can remind everyone who has ever been to any past Programming Council event. It may not sound like much at first, but at the end of the first year, you should have a list of over one thousand people who are interested in these events.

✔   Find out what you're doing right, and what you're doing wrong. For example, at the University of St. Thomas in Houston, at the end of each event, nobody is allowed to leave until they have filled out an opinion card. Make sure to ask how they found out about the event, what they liked, what they didn't like, and what they'd like to see changed.

✔   Make sure to listen to your audience. From a demographic standpoint, nobody is more likely to come to your next event than those who came to the last one. When you collect their suggestions, treat them like gold.

✔   Do everything you can to have your current audiences come back next time. In advertising terms, make sure you have a strong base of "repeat customers."

24. MAKE IT CYBER

Okay, so we mentioned an email list, which brings up the next issue: a campus activities web site. Yours can be as fancy or as sparse as you'd like, but there is one very important rule: update regularly. Nothing is as frustrating as a web site that was last updated a year ago. This renders your web site useless and guarantees that nobody will go to it.

At the very least, your site should have an accurate calendar of events, including each act, the date of each show, time of each show, and location of the event. Once you have this down, you can add value to your web site and increase traffic by adding:

EXAMPLES:

✔   A Bulletin Board for comments about events. You can get one at http://www.ultimatebb.com/

✔   Preview pages for each upcoming act, including links to each act's web site.

✔   A signup section to join your campus activities email list.

25.

Think like P.T. Barnum - the most outrageous marketer who's ever lived. He'd "humbug" the audience with things like the Fejee Mermaid - an elaborate hoax, claimed to be a cross between a monkey and a fish. The public was permitted to see the mermaid "FREE OF CHARGE!" (provided they paid admission to walk through Barnum's museum to reach it). Of course he tricked them in to coming, but then provided so much value for their time and money, nobody thought to complain.

If you make the "gotcha" fun and clever enough, people enjoy the ruse. You still want to give them something of value, but you can "over exaggerate" in the name of a Humbug!

For example, a store owner in Australia promised his customers that if he sold 100 topcoats on a particular day he would walk "buck naked" through the center of town. Hundreds of people showed up, and he sold his quota of coats (and then some). At last, he kept his word by walking a beautiful dog named "Buck Naked" through the center of town. He lived up to his promise and everyone got a good laugh out of the stunt. Think creatively!

EXAMPLES:

✔   Advertise that at your show you're giving away "five chances to win $1000.00." Then give away five lottery tickets.

✔   Advertise FREE dinners given to the first 150 people through the door. Then buy a couple of cases of Ramen noodles (about a nickel apiece in the case lots) and give them away. It's the perfect College Meal and you'll get the campus talking and pack the house at the same time.

✔   Advertise a FREE puppy given away during the show. Then give away a balloon dog.

✔   In promoting their latest boxing game at the Electronic Entertainment Expo, game maker Electronic Arts placed large posters advertising personal appearances and a boxing match between legends Sugar Ray Leonard and Oscar De La Hoya. Sure enough, there was even a large boxing ring set up at EA's booth. When it was time for the fight, music blasted and both fighters emerged in boxing trunks. Finally, both legends walked up to the Sony Playstation and began playing the new boxing game, each using the virtual boxer modeled on themselves!

✔   In Tulsa, Oklahoma, Billboards advertising a hotel-based bar proclaimed "COME SEE OUR 60-FOOT INDOOR WATERFALL!" Inside the bar was in fact a huge waterfall--60 feet long and one foot high!

✔   Despair.com made a name for itself by creating parody "demotivator" posters that encouraged office workers to lower their expectations and give up their dreams. As an interesting publicity stunt, Despair sought to trademark the "frowny face" moticon. :-(

Amazingly (and much to their surprise), they were granted the trademark, and in a brilliant humbug, announced that they would initiate a multi-trillion dollar lawsuit against EVERYONE WHO EVER USED THE FROWNY FACE! Of course the lawsuit was a gag, but it did generate front-page headlines for the business, and brought them valuable exposure.

✔   At Millikin University in Decatur, Illinois, posters around campus advertised a "TOPLESS CAR WASH," sponsored by Pi Phi sorority. The posters declared "come see what all the fuss is about!" and "5 dollars for these lovely ladies to scrub your car!" Of course, these ladies kept their promise: at the event they would clean each car. . . except for the top!

✔   It is crucially important that this be done in good fun and as a joke. Have fun with it, actually deliver on your promises, but in a funny and unexpected way, and everyone will enjoy being "humbugged".

26. MAKE IT TODAY

Run a "day of the event campaign." You should think of the events you are promoting on campus as having two separate marketing campaigns: The first campaign is making everyone aware that the event is happening. The second campaign is letting everyone know the event is happening TODAY.

Remember there are *hundreds* of people who want to come to your event... they just haven't been forced into making the mental decision to commit their time. This is your day to change all those "think-it-overs" into attendees.

Students live busy lives and unless you remind them of your event, they may have the best intentions of coming to your event, but simply forget. Jog their memories with some of these ideas.

EXAMPLES:

✔   Northwestern State University in Louisiana keeps a stack of florescent orange bumper stickers with the word "TODAY" printed on it. On the day of every event the programming board hosts, they put the stickers on every poster promoting the event. It both changes the way the poster looks and reminds people to come to the event.

✔   John Carroll University in Ohio gave fortune cookies to every student who went through the cafeteria line the day of a hypnosis show. Each fortune read "There is a hypnosis show in your future" and gave the information about show time & date.

✔   Use sidewalk chalk to remind students about the event... and draw arrows to where the event is taking place!

✔   Make your own "Event tonight: ask me about it!" T-shirts and buttons. Have everyone in your programming board wear them on the day of every event. It's amazing how many people will ask about the event.

✔   Use helium filled balloons with "event tonight" and your program board logo printed on them every time you have an event. This type of regular notice acts as a "beacon," reminding students about events they may not have realized were that day.

✔   Always send E-mail reminders of the event to your e-mail list. Send the e-mail first thing in the morning (or even the night before) so it's likely to be read by the most people.

✔   Use day-of-the-event teasers, lectures, and workshops to remind students of the performance or event that night.

✔   Radio spots. If you have campus radio or TV, make sure that you post reminders on these. You can even schedule the artist for an interview if they are available; if they're not, then just send someone from the programming board for FREE publicity.

✔   Set up the stage or performance area early in the day! Never underestimate the power of curiosity. When students see a platform being set up, they will often ask what's happening and realize that the event they've heard so much about is happening tonight! Put a banner or sign near the stage with the answer to the questions of "Who, When, and Where."

27. MAKE IT

Risqué

There's a reason for the old saying, "Sex sells." Whether humorous, tasteful, or outrageous, try using light-hearted, funny, and slightly risqué ways to get your promotional messages read.

For Example, several billboards currently advertise "CLOTHING OPTIONAL ONLINE DEFENSIVE DRIVING." Many people find themselves re-reading the message two or three times before fully understanding it. Of course, that's exactly what advertisers want!

At Texas A&M, students promoted their upcoming "Big Event" by running a series of classified ads featuring fictional quotes from celebrities about the "Big Event." One such quote read "'It's the third biggest thing I've ever seen!' - Dolly Parton."

Of course, remember that you CAN go to far with this technique. You want to grab people's attention without offending any potential attendees of your event. Make sure to run your ideas by any appropriate university officials before posting them around campus (with risqué material, it IS better to ask permission than to beg forgiveness).

EXAMPLES:

✔   Stephen F. Austin University brought in a juggler with a very unique signature effect, which used rolls of toilet paper. To grab people's attention, program board members placed large signs inside each bathroom stall with arrows that pointed to the toilet paper. Each sign read "Guess what our juggler does with THIS!"

✔   In the mid-eighties, Stroh's beer assembled a group of bikini clad women, gave them blonde wigs, taught them to speak with heavy accents, and renamed them the "Swedish Bikini Team." These women appeared on TV, in magazines, and on calendars, all while promoting Stroh's beer! You can assemble your own group of parading women (and men!) in bathing suits, perhaps carrying signs for your event.

✔   When promoting a bizarre magician who promised to

hammer a 4.5 inch nail in his nose, Eastern New Mexico University handed out nails with an attached slightly suggestive message: "guess where our magician is going to stick <u>this</u>?!"

✔   While promoting an event with a Scottish theme, one university dressed up a mannequin with traditional Scottish garb, complete with kilt. When students walked into the room, they would often see other students peeking under the mannequin's kilt and laughing as they walked off. Curious, each student would sheepishly peek under the kilt, only to discover a flier advertising the upcoming event!

✔   Many morning radio shows have custom-made urinal filters with risqué slogans. Think of ways to adapt these ideas to your events, using a little "potty humor."

28. MAKE IT Mobile

We live an a mobile society. People eat, drink, visit, talk on the phone and more (see number 27) in their cars. Take advantage of this knowledge and hit people where they live in their cars, on their bikes, walking and on the bus.

EXAMPLES:

✔ The University of Texas at the Permian Basin puts big, two sided signs in the beds of pick up trucks announcing upcoming events. In the parking lots, driving around campus and driving around town - these mobile billboards get noticed.

✔ Henderson State University in Arkansas has a large bulletin board on wheels announcing their newest upcoming event that they put in front of major events, sporting events, and public places. They move this board to wherever the most people will be on any given day.

✔ Most schools have some sort of a bus system. Work it out with the transportation department to put your ads on the bus. Students have nothing else to do while riding the bus and they will read what you've written.

✔ If you can't get on the bus - then use the bus stop as a place to advertise your event. Again, you'll catch people who have nothing else to do.

✔ For a few dollars at a party goods store you can get "window paint" for your vehicle. The kind used to paint windows at a wedding. Use the programming boards vehicles as moving billboards for your upcoming event. This will serve as a great reminder about the event.

✔ A lot of students ride bikes to class. If you can get your message on or near the bike racks you'll get more attention.

29. MAKE IT parasitic

Although you should do everything you can to promote your event, sometimes you can take advantage of unique situations or other events to help boost attendance at yours. Look around your campus and try to find events or activities that already draw students, and try to think of ways to pull that same crowd over to your event (without disturbing the other event, of course).

One very direct example of this technique was applied by Graceland University in Lamoni, Iowa. They placed posters around campus that read "Did you like the regurgitator? Then you'll love this bizarre magician!" In effect, they were able to capture the enthusiasm for a previous event and redirect it to their latest incoming event.

EXAMPLES:

✔   Albertson College of Idaho was in a jam. They had already booked their magic show for a specific date and time, only to discover that a major basketball game was scheduled for the same night! Knowing that they couldn't convince students to attend the show instead of the basketball game, they decided to turn the game itself into an advertisement for the magic show.

They began by changing the official time of the show to "after the game" on all promotional items. Then, during the game, they tossed candies out with attached messages detailing the show's content, time, and location. On top of that, announcements advertising the show were read four times during the game. The end result was that almost the entire crowd went directly from the game to the magic show!

✔   Every campus usually has a cluster of public computers with internet access, usually in an academic center or microcomputer facility. You can reach students by getting permission to set every computer's home page as an advertisement for your event! This way, not only will students be notified of your upcoming event, but can have a chance to read reviews, watch video, and more!

For an extra kick, ask your incoming event for a CD-ROM filled with promotional pictures, ad copy, video and copies of their web site. Then, you can use these assets to create a more powerful presentation.

✔   Work out an arrangement with your residence halls to allow you to place fliers in every mailbox in the hall. Follow up with custom-made door hanger advertisements. Not only will you catch students where they live, but the repeat exposure will get your message out.

At Indiana University in Pennsylvania, the programming board worked out a deal with dorms to put signs in their windows promoting each upcoming event. These signs would spell out the event name across the windows and each floor would create a new line!

✔   Try working out an arrangement with several classes to offer extra-credit to students attending your events, or perhaps even make their attendance mandatory as part of a related class project. This is actually easier than you might think.

Psychology classes should attend hypnosis shows. Speech classes can attend your public speaking events. Theatre classes can be made to attend novelty shows, including jugglers, magicians, and comedians, to focus on each act's use of staging and theatrics. Music classes might be asked to attend a visiting musician or band, to critique each performance. Film students must attend your movie screenings. Advertising students can get extra credit for analyzing your council's use of promotional materials and publicity stunts. The possibilities are endless!

30. MAKE IT complimentary

Do the acts you book work well together? Do you have an ongoing theme in your programming? Do you make one event promote the next event?   You should. Anytime you can tie your programming events together, you'll end up with more people at your events.

Southwest Texas State University had an upcoming production featuring real pro-wrestling action, provided by Extreme Texas Wrestling. To boost interest in the event, SWT staged an interruption of another of their own events! During this seemingly unrelated event, one wrestler charged the stage and challenged another. The costumed loudmouth certainly captured everyone's attention (and interest), and the drama played out the following week at the actual wrestling match.

EXAMPLES:

✔ Use events that compliment one another. This works especially well with films. Have an inflatable "Titanic" sinking ship slide to promote the film of the same name. Book the oversized Sumo Wrestler outfits to promote a martial arts film. Host a game show with a film theme to promote the entire film series.

✔ Consider booking an opening act for your larger events. Remember, this doesn't have to be another touring show, but could be a homegrown gameshow, a local musician, or a popular on-campus performer.

✔ Create a serial drama, similar to the stage-rushing incident at SWT (above). People may show up to events just to find out what happens next!

✔ One way to tie your events together is to have students sign up for a drawing at one event and announce the winner at the next event! Of course, this works best when the winner must be present to win. Note: announce the winner at the END of the event.

31. MAKE IT ENVIRONMENTAL

Creating a special environment or theme for your event can simply transform a standard event into a true campus happening. Use this theme in creating your advertising, decorating for an event, AND in choosing the right acts.

Austin College in Sherman, Texas fundamentally changed the nature of their movie presentation by showing The Blair Witch Project in the middle of the woods, projected onto a sheet tied between two trees.

Likewise, Shenandoah College in Westminster, West Virginia showed a "dive-in" theatre production of Jaws in the swimming pool. As an added twist, their SCUBA club swam around the bottom of the pool the whole time, occasionally grabbing ankles at particularly tense moments.

EXAMPLES:

✔ Decorate the entrance to your events, based on the appropriate theme. This is easy at Halloween, Christmas, Easter, etc., but try to think of unusual decorations for other events.

✔   For a Jimmy Buffet type singer, you might transform your cafeteria into a tropical island, complete with construction-paper palm trees and styrofoam coconuts.

✔   If you're featuring a family or children's entertainer, consider booking a giant chair and photographer, to "bring out the kid" in each college student and add to the ambience of the event (see number 30).

✔   Don't just hand out fliers for your event; try dressing your programming council as outrageously themed costume characters. THEN have them hand out fliers!

32. MAKE IT

VARIED

Take a look around your campus and pay close attention to what types of advertising are being overused. Now make sure you don't follow suit! Don't let YOUR advertising blend in with the crowd - stand out from it!

Rely on several different tactics and advertisement methods to get your event noticed. Each person who comes to your event will do so for a completely different reason. Take advantage of this by advertising as many different aspects of your event as you can, in as drastically different styles as possible.

One great example of this tactic was applied by Skagit Valley College in Washington. Rather than hang their posters on the walls, they attached them to ribbons dangling from helium-filled balloons up on the ceiling. Each flier hung at eye-level, so they were impossible to miss!

EXAMPLES:

✔   Use different size and color papers - 8 ½ x 11 is VERY overused and seems to get less noticed.

✔   Try creating advertisements for extremely off-sized paper. For example, print two ads on an 11 x 17 sheet and then cut it in half LENGTHWISE. The unique size makes it different.   Different gets it noticed.

✔   Try creating advertisements that look nothing like adver- tisements. In other words, try disguising your message with drab, plain times new roman font and the headline "public notice," "important update," "final opportunity," "warning," or even "for sale!"

✔   Put small posters on vending machines. Students use vending machines for everything from soft drinks to dinner. Put your postcard sized message near the coin slot and you'll be cashing in on each sale too!

✔   Remember also that not only do different types of adver- tising work well for different students, but also that different REASONS for attending the event affect different students. In the audience at a single magic show, you'll find individuals who came for the mind-reading, just for the comedy, or just because they saw the performer on national television.

Remember that you should create SEPARATE ADVERTISEMENTS for each type of person you want to attract to your show. The same advertisement, word for word, will be more effective if it is split into 10 different versions: one with unicorns, one with fire, one with computers, one with the word "sex!", and so on. Keep in mind that the only thing your customers care about is themselves, and unless you mention something that THEY are interested in, they probably won't know how great your event is.

✔   A good rule of thumb is to imagine that each different type of advertisement will bring in 10% of your total crowd. Try to think of 10 totally different angles (not just methods) to promote each event, and you'll end up with stronger attendance.

Just as we've seen a lot of schools do things right, we've seen a lot of problems keep schools from getting the most out of their events. Lucky for you, we've been keeping notes, and have discovered...

The 10

Deadly Mistakes

Made by Event Promoters

1. **Failing to think of your students as your customers.** Whether your events are free or pay-per-ticket, the success of campus events depends largely on ONE factor: attendance. Remember that hiring the best acts in the business is USELESS unless your students turn out for the event. Thinking in terms of capturing and retaining customers will help you to focus on the importance of your advertising and marketing. After all, we can all survive without students, but NO enterprise can do without CUSTOMERS.

2. **Not <u>listening</u> to your customers**. Evaluations can reshape your events and programs in ways you currently cannot even imagine. Every successful programming board collects and reads evaluations after every event. Every unsuccessful programming board does not. Your evaluations should tell you not only what your crowds thought of each act (making it easy to decide who comes back next year), but also how they found out about the show, why they came, and what YOU can do to get them to come back.

3. **Not keeping your current customers coming back.** Absolutely nobody is more likely to come to your next event than those who attended your previous event. Therefore, it should make lots of sense to cater to this crowd. What events draw your biggest turnouts? If you find that musicians bring in your students, perhaps you should hire more musicians. If hypnosis brings in the crowd, hire more hypnotists. Don't presume to dictate what your students should and should not be excited about. Instead, make sure YOU bend to their desires.

4. **Not asking for help.** You have limited time and resources to market each of your events. Rather than reinvent the wheel each week, make sure to take advantage of existing resources, especially those that come from the act themselves. While you're promoting the show for the first time, THEY have been promoting the same show for years and years. In addition to promotional materials, your acts should provide you with detailed explanations of what has and has not worked in the past when promoting their show. Many acts have created custom guides, detailing how best you can tailor your promotion to their show.

5. Not taking advantage of electronic media.
While most programming boards have a web site, very few use them effectively. Your web site should ALWAYS be up to date, including a "what's new" section that's never more than a week old. This will keep your site full of interesting, compelling content that will keep your customers coming back. However, FAR more important than any web site is an active E-mail list of your current customers. These addresses can be very easily collected in your evaluations, or by simply passing around a clipboard before the show. By the end of your first semester, you can have hundreds or even thousands of TARGETED E-mail addresses, allowing you to remind everyone about your events the night before.

6. Scheduling your event opposite another competing event. Do your research. Double-check community calendars, sports calendars, concert calendars, etc. to make sure that your students are free to

attend your event. Check for long weekends, exam times, Greek events, housing events and any other potential competition. After all, your customers can only be in one place at a time.

7. Failing to take initiative in promoting your event.
If it's three weeks before your event and you still have not received any promo materials from your act, take the initiative to call them and find out what's going on. Or better yet, go to the act's web site and start producing your own in-house promotional materials. What you must NEVER do is sit back and assume that people will attend an event they know nothing about.

8. Not being complete and specific in your advertising.
Many programmers fall into the trap of wanting their advertising to look good, rather than be effective. Remember that every single advertisement (unless it is intentionally designed to be mysterious) should cover Who, What, When, Why and Where and provide a way to learn more about the event (usually a web site link, phone number or place to obtain tickets/ reservations).

9. Not attending the event yourself.
Why should your students care about an event that you won't

make the time to attend yourself? Make sure that you are enthusiastic about every event you bring to campus. You'll find that your excitement is infectious, and will result in greater attendance.

10. Not creating habits and value early in the year.
Incoming freshman and transfer students will quickly fall into habits as they enter a new school. If you don't condition them early in their college career to attend programming events, you may never capture these customers. Start the year off with a sure fire hit (especially one you've had before) while the students have nothing competing for their attention. Then, keep them coming back for more by having regular events and teasing your next show at the end of each current show, using announcements, reservations, special privilege sign ups, fliers, and more.